All about coffee

Brew Your Coffee Knowledge

Table of Contents

Prologue

Coffee is termed as the drink of choice around the world. Often associated with energy and alertness. But lets be honest, its actually about its tentalizing taste and soothing aroma. It is rightly said that "Life begins after a cup of Coffee".

I am Lenny Peake and being a coffee fiend myself; I never miss my daily stop at a local coffeeshop in the morning, the afternoon and the evening. Plus, a visit or two in between! And not surprisingly, I often find myself browsing some short notes or articles on the internet. Pulling in tidbits of coffee knowledge; while sipping in a hot cup of coffee, acts like a subtle taste enhancer. So I thought would be helpful to take some of these more interesting articles and compile a short eBook that would summarize the more important and interesting facts of coffee culture and history. I do hope you get some intersting information from this book....and more importantly... enjoy it !

Disclaimer

The information contained in this book and its contents is not designed to replace or take the place of any form of medical or professional advice; and is not meant to replace the need for independent medical, financial, legal or other professional advice or services, as may be required. The content and information in this book has been provided for educational and entertainment purposes only.

The content and information contained in this book has been compiled from sources deemed reliable, and it is accurate to the best of the Author's knowledge, information and belief. However, the Author cannot guarantee its accuracy and validity and cannot be held liable for any errors and/or omissions. Further, changes are periodically made to this book as and when needed.

Upon using the contents and information contained in this book, you agree to hold harmless the Author from and against any damages, costs, and expenses, including any legal fees potentially resulting from the application of any of the information provided by this book. This disclaimer applies to any loss, damages or injury caused by the use and application, whether directly or indirectly, of any advice or information presented, whether for breach of contract, tort, negligence, personal injury, criminal intent, or under any other cause of action.

You agree that by continuing to read this book, where appropriate and/or necessary, you shall consult a professional (including but not limited to your doctor, attorney, or financial advisor or such other advisor as needed) before using any of the suggested remedies, techniques, or information in this book.

Part - I

List of Topics

Coffee - The Drink of Choice

Did you know coffee is the most consumed beverage in the world. How did coffee get this ranking? What country first figured out coffee was safe for consumption? When was the first drink of coffee prepared? Where did the first coffee shop come in being?

There are many questions about the starting point of drinking coffee. It has been so long ago no one really knows all the facts. But, one thing is for sure, coffee is the most consumed beverage on the planet.

The Beginning of Coffee

It looks as if the first trace came out of Abyssinia and was also sporadically in the vicinity of the Red Sea around seven hundred AD. Along with these people, other Africans of the same period also have a history of using the coffee berry pulp for more than one occasion like rituals and even for health. Coffee began to get more attention when the Arabs began cultivating it in their peninsulas around eleven hundred AD. It is speculated that trade ships brought the coffee their way. The Arabs started making a drink that became quite popular called gahwa--- meaning to prevent sleep. Roasting and boiling the bean was how they made this drink. It became so popular among the Arabs that they made it their signature Arabian wine and it was used a lot during rituals. After the coffee bean was found to be a great wine and a medicine, someone discovered in Arabia that you could also make a different dark, delicious drink out of the beans, this happened somewhere around twelve hundred AD. After that it didn't take long and everyone in Arabia was drinking coffee. Everywhere these people traveled the coffee went with them. It made its way around to India, North Africa, the eastern Mediterranean, and was then cultivated to a great extent in Yemen around fourteen hundred AD. Other countries would have gladly welcomed these beans if only the Arabs had let them. The Arabs killed the seed-germ making sure no one else could grow the coffee if taken elsewhere. Heavily guarding their plants, Yemen is where the main source of coffee stayed for several hundred years. Even with their efforts, the beans were eventually smuggled out by pilgrims and travelers.

Discovering the Coffee

There are a few circulating stories about the discovery of the effects of coffee and its initial consumption. They all revolve around an Ethiopian goat herder called Kaldi. It's said on one fateful day Kaldi noticed goats in his heard behaving inordinately energetically. On further observation he linked their behaviour with red berries growing on some bushes which they were seen eating.

Curious; he tried the berries and found he too began to feel animated. It wasn't long before he shared this new discovery with others and the berries became popular throughout the land. It's not known if Kaldi was a member of the Galla tribe in Ethiopia but they are said to have consumed a mixture of ground berries and animal fat earlier than 1000AD.

Arab traders soon encountered coffee in their travels bringing it back to their homelands and cultivating the plant on farms. It was these Arab traders around 1000AD who were also likely to be the first to have boiled the beans consuming them as a drink identified for its ability to prevent sleep.

Bernard Lewis, in his "Istanbul and the Civilization of the Ottoman Empire", tells of the ottoman scribe Ä°brahim Peçevi who wrote of the first coffeehouse in Istanbul: "Until the year 1555, in the High, God-Guarded city of Constantinople, as well as in Ottoman lands generally, coffee and coffee-houses did not exist. About that year, a fellow called Hakam from Aleppo and a wag called Shams from Damascus came to the city; they each opened a large shop in the district called Tahtakale, and began to purvey coffee."

The demand for coffee around this time escalated to such importance that soon it was legally acceptable for a woman to divorce her husband if he was not able to supply her with her daily coffee.

Around 150 years later coffee was introduced to Italy by Italian traders. Although initially declared an infidel threat by the Vatican in fear of Ottoman influence, Pope Clement the VIII after no doubt tasting the drink himself was quick to declare it acceptable for Christian consumption. In 1645 the first of what would be many coffeehouses opened in Italy.

In 1650 the fist coffee house in England The Grand Cafe is alleged to have been opened in Oxford. The café exists to this day though their specialty is now wine. Soon thereafter more and more cafes began to open around England. They became a place to share ideas and news of the day. It was from here the term 'Penny Universities' was coined. A penny was the price of admission, an affordable sum, which allowed the well to do to share ideas with those who were less fortunate. Two years later, a Greek from Ragusa named Pascal Rosea opened the first coffeehouse in London, in Cornhill. In 1668 Edward Lloyd opened his famous Coffee House in Lombard Street, London, which soon became a popular congregation for shipowners and sea merchants.

1668 was a pivotal year in coffees adaptation into north American culture as this was the year that New York City's favourite breakfast drink beer was replaced by coffee.

Pascal Rosea after opening the first coffee house in London also established the first coffee house in Paris France in 1672. The café stood alone as a coffee outlet in the city until Café Procope opened in 1686. Café Procope is still in existence and boasts a history of being the gathering place of historic figures such as Voltaire, Denis Diderot and Rousseau. Café Procope will also argue it's right as the birthplace of the Encyclopédie, the first modern encyclopedia.

Europe's first Viennese café is commonly accepted as being opened by a Greek merchant named Ioannis Diodato in 1675. It was coffee houses in Vienna that established the process of filtering out the coffee grounds adding sugar and milk. A vienna coffee is one prepared with cream, this perhaps a throwback to Viennese influence.

It was circa 1690 that the coffee plant was smuggled out of the Arab port of Mocha by the Dutch and transported and farmed in new colonies in Ceylon and Java. Java is now a well known bean origin.

The mayor of Amsterdam gave Louis XIV of France a small coffee bush as a gift in 1714. Louis XIV treasured the tree highly and had it tended to in his royal greenhouses. Years later in 1723 a French

Captain who; whilst visiting from his station in Martinique managed to convince the kings physician to source a cutting from the bush. His intention was to cultivate coffee on the lush volcanic island of Martinique. This cutting may very well have seen up to 90% of the world's coffee originating from this plant and it almost didn't make it to Martinique due to rough seas, attempted theft and pirates. Fifty years later there were 19 million coffee trees which were noted in an official survey.

1727 was a pivotal chapter in the proliferation of the coffee tree. It was in this year in Guianna; at a time of border disputes between France and Holland, a Lieutenant Colonel Francisco de Melo Palheta manages to smuggle a plant from the French. During his time there arbitrating the dispute, the colonel became involved with the French governor's wife. At the time of their parting the governor's wife presented to him a bouquet of flowers which also contained coffee tree clippings and seeds. Lieutenant Colonel Francisco de Melo Palheta returned to Brasil introducing on his arrival the coffee tree. Brazil would unbeknownst to him at the time, become in years to come the largest producer of coffee in the world.

In 1773 it was declared at Boston Harbour in the US that it shall be every American's patriotic duty to drink coffee. After heavy taxes were imposed on tea exported to America, colonists in the new nation began a revolt by throwing tea into the Boston Harbour, thus the name 'Boston Tea Party'. This action by the Boston Tea Party not only set the wheels in motion for the revolution but it also led to the adaptation of coffee as America's choice drink.

On August 11 1903 Satori Kato a Japanese Chemist working in the US filed for patent the "Coffee Concentrate and Process of Making Same," the first patent for instant coffee. That is not to say water soluble coffee was not in existence at the time, although it had a very short shelf life and went rancid very quickly. It was due to this that the idea of instant coffee disappeared as soon as it emerged prior to Satori Kato. In his April 1901 patent application Satori Kato explains the problem and how he solved it: " The volatile oil is mixed with the solid aqueous extract, but I have discovered that an attempt to effect this without other precaution results in the production of a pasty sticky mass which does not resist rancidity, but quickly spoils under the usual conditions of transportation and storage. I have further discovered that the difficulty arises from the presence of in the concentrate of the non-volatile coffee-fat or at any rate is overcome by its removal, which, I believe, I am the first to effect. I separate the volatile oil and the fats from the coffee and remove the fibre and reduce to a hard substance. This hard substance is reduced to a finely divided condition and a portion thereof is pulverized and thoroughly mixed with the pure volatile oil and dried, after which this mixture is mixed with the remainder of the hard substance and used in this granulated or flaky form or pressed into tablets."

In Germany around this time Ludwig Roselius a German Coffee Merchant develops the first commercially successful decaffeination process in Bremen Germany with his assistant Karl Kimmer. This process used benzene or methylene chloride as a solvent to remove the caffeine. Ludwig Roselius founded the brand Sanka to market his decaffeinated beans. Today the use of

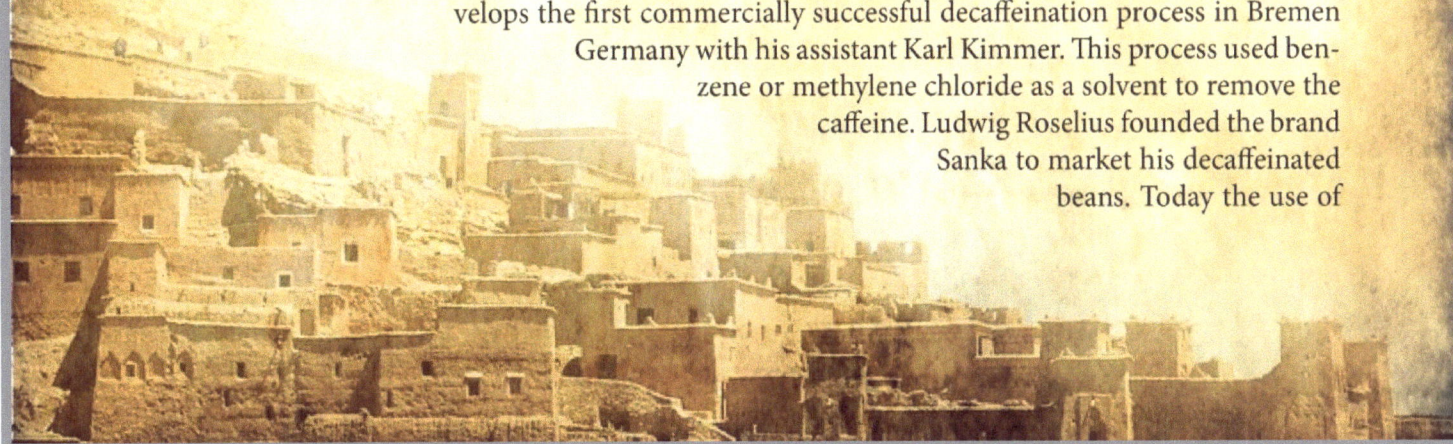

chemicals to remove caffeine is no longer in use.

Another inventor, Englishman George Constant Washington, living in Guatemala noticed powdery coffee build-up on the spout of his coffee carafe, He soon goes on to develop his own instant coffee and mass-produces his brand Red E Coffee in 1906. Red E Coffee was procured as rations for US troops during World War I. Nescafe soon developed an improved process and started marketing their brand in 1938. They went on to supply the US military with coffee rations during World War II. By 1940 the US was importing up to 70 percent of the worlds coffee harvest.

Achilles Gaggia and The Birth Of Modern Espresso The Gaggia story begins with Mrs Rosetta Scorza, the wife of Sr. Cremonese a coffee grinder technician in Milan who patented the idea of a screw piston which forced water through coffee in the 1930s. When Cremonese died leaving Rosetta Scorza with the patent she was largely unsuccessful in interesting manufacturers with the design.

We can assume Gaggia a bar owner was perhaps approached by Rosetta, as we know in 1938 Gaggia lodged a patent application for a piston mechanism doing largely the same thing as the Cremonese patent. Gaggia went on to further develop and patent a screw piston forged from aluminium and brass, the distinct difference this time is that he had connected this system to a boiler. Gaggia experimented with various styles and materials including surprisingly asbestos in an effort regulate temperature. Gaggia's design did encroach on Rosetta Scorza's patent and led to Gaggia making a payment in using the design.

Gaggia went on in 1947 to patent a spring operated lever and piston mechanism which was totally different to previous patents, this paved the way for pressurised coffee and the machines we know of today. This new patent allowed for pressurised water pushed through the coffee independently of the pressure in the boiler, it also allowed the temperature to be regulated with a quicker and stronger extraction. Gaggia was now producing coffee unlike any other seen or tasted before, his extraction process was producing a rich golden crema, and perhaps he was a little unsure of it himself, but being the salesman he was, he wasted no time in installing his machines in bars and advertising the product with a sign on the window saying "Caffe crema di caffe natural" - coffee cream from natural coffee.

From there the adoption of the new style coffee gained momentum and soon Gaggia was exporting his machines worldwide aiding in the proliferation of espresso coffee all over the world.

Coffee Shops & Coffee Tips

Around 1475 the first coffee shop opens in Constantinople called Kiv Han two years after coffee was introduced to Turkey, in 1554 two coffee houses open there. People came pouring in to socialize, listen to music, play games and of course drink coffee. Some often called these places in Turkey the "school of the wise", because you could learn so much by just visiting the coffee house and listening to conversations. In the sixteen hundreds coffee enters Europe through the port of Venice. The Turkish warriors also brought the drink to Balkans, Spain, and North Africa. Not too much later the first coffee house opens in Italy. There were plenty of people also trying to ban coffee. Such as Khair Beg a governor of Mecca who was executed and Grand Vizir of the Ottoman Empire who successfully closed down many coffee houses in Turkey. Thankfully not everyone thought this way.

In the early sixteen hundreds coffee is presented to the New World by man named John Smith. Later in that century, the first coffee house opens in England. Coffee houses or "penny universities" charged a penny for admission and for a cup of coffee. The word "TIPS" (for service) has it's origin from an English coffee house. Early in the 17th century, Edward Lloyd's coffee house opens in England. The Dutch became the first to commercially transport coffee. The first Parisian café opens in 1713 and King Louis XIV is presented with a lovely coffee tree. Sugar is first used as an addition to coffee in his court.

"Brew" in the 20th Century

New methods to help brewing coffee start popping up everywhere. The first commercial espresso machine is developed in Italy. Melitta Bentz makes a filter using blotting paper. Dr. Ernest Lily manufactures the first automatic espresso machine. The Nestle Company invents Nescafe instant coffee. Achilles Gaggia perfects the espresso machine. Hills Bros. begins packing roasted coffee in vacuum tins eventually ending local roasting shops and coffee mills. A Japanese-American chemist named Satori Kato from Chicago invents the first soluble "instant" coffee. German coffee importer Ludwig Roselius turns some ruined coffee beans over to researchers, who perfected the process of removing caffeine from the beans without destroying the flavor. He sells it under the name Sanka. Sanka is introduced in the United States in 1923. George Constant Washington an English chemist living in Guatemala, is interested in a powdery condensation forming on the spout of his silver coffee flask. After checking into it, he creates the first mass-produced instant coffee which is his brand name called Red E Coffee. Prohibition goes into effect in United States. Coffee sales suddenly increase. Brazil asked Nestle to help find a solution to their coffee surpluses so the Nestle Company comes up with freeze-dried coffee. Nestle also made Nescafe and introduced it to Switzerland.

Interesting Coffee Tidbits

Today the US imports 70 percent of the world's coffee crop.

During W.W.II, American soldiers were issued instant Maxwell House coffee in their ration kits.

In 1938; Italy, Achilles Gaggia perfects his espresso machine.

The name Cappuccino comes from the resemblance of its color to the robes of the monks of the Capuchin order.

One week before Woodstock, the Manson family murders coffee heiress Abigail Folger as she visits with her friend Sharon Tate in the home of filmmaker Roman Polanski.

Coffee plants were introduced in the America's on the island of O'ahu, Hawaii in the early 1800's. This century also had a vast amount of time spent on developing better methods for brewing coffee. By close to the end of the seventeen hundreds, 1,920 million plants are grown on the island. Evidently the eighteen hundreds were spent trying to find better methods to make coffee.

Starbucks opens its first store in Seattle's Pike Place public market in 1971. This creates madness over fresh-roasted whole bean coffee. Coffee finally becomes the world's most popular beverage. More than 450 billion cups are sold each year by 1995.

Now in the 21st century we have many different styles, grinds, and flavors of coffee. We have really come a long way even with our coffee making machines. There's no sign of coffee consumption decreasing. Researchers are even finding many health benefits to drinking coffee. Drink and enjoy!

Part - II

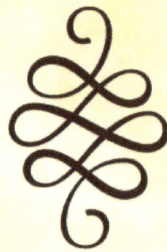

List of Topics

Coffee Life

Caffeine in Coffee - Good or Bad?

Coffee - Healthy for the Liver?

Coffee and Physical Fitness

Any Negative Effects of Coffee?

Coffee Life

Many of us rely on coffee to get us going in the mornings, wake us up in the afternoons, and prepare us for that special business meeting. Go ahead, have a cup of coffee. It's much healthier than you may be thinking right now. Coffee is the most consumed beverage in the world. No matter where you go, coffee is usually available. Yet, until recently there's been very little research on the effects of coffee on our health. The researcher's are waking up however. There have recently been studies completed on a variety of health benefits to drinking that simply delicious cup of coffee. In a study in Italy, it was proven that that brewed coffee contains many antioxidants and consumption of antioxidant-rich brewed coffee may inhibit diseases caused by oxidative damages. When compared to other caffeine containing beverages like tea and cocoa, coffee proved to be the best in helping to prevent disease.

Caffeine in Coffee - Good or Bad?

The caffeine in coffee has often been a source of concern for many. Most people have problems sleeping when they drink coffee right before bedtime. Others will drink coffee to give them that boost of energy caffeine provides. Some even feel their heart rate increase if they drink too much coffee. Did you know there are also benefits to the caffeine found in coffee? Coffee intake (due to the caffeine) was associated with a significantly lower risk for Alzheimer's Disease, independently of other possible confounding variables. These results, with future prospective studies, may have a major impact on the prevention of Alzheimer's disease. Another benefit of drinking coffee has been studied in China. Their research clinically proved the caffeine in coffee helps to prevent Parkinson's disease. Many of us have been led to believe that caffeine is bad for us. True enough, large quantities may hurt us, but the evidence is strong for the benefits it provides.

Coffee - Healthy for the Liver?

Studies completed in Japan indicated that people who drink more than a cup of coffee a day are less likely to develop liver cancer than those who do not, Japanese researchers say. Coffee also helped lower the risk of cirrhosis of the liver. Chlorogenic acid present in coffee beans has been proven in studies to also reduce the risk of liver cancer. Harvard Medical School completed a study in 2004 that strongly suggest coffee has preventative qualities for Type 2 diabetes and insulin resistance. The authors found an inverse association between coffee intake and type 2 diabetes after adjustment for age, body mass index, and other risk factors. Total caffeine intake from coffee and other sources was associated with a statistically significantly lower risk for diabetes in both men and women. These data suggest that long-term coffee consumption is associated with a statistically significantly lower risk for type 2 diabetes.

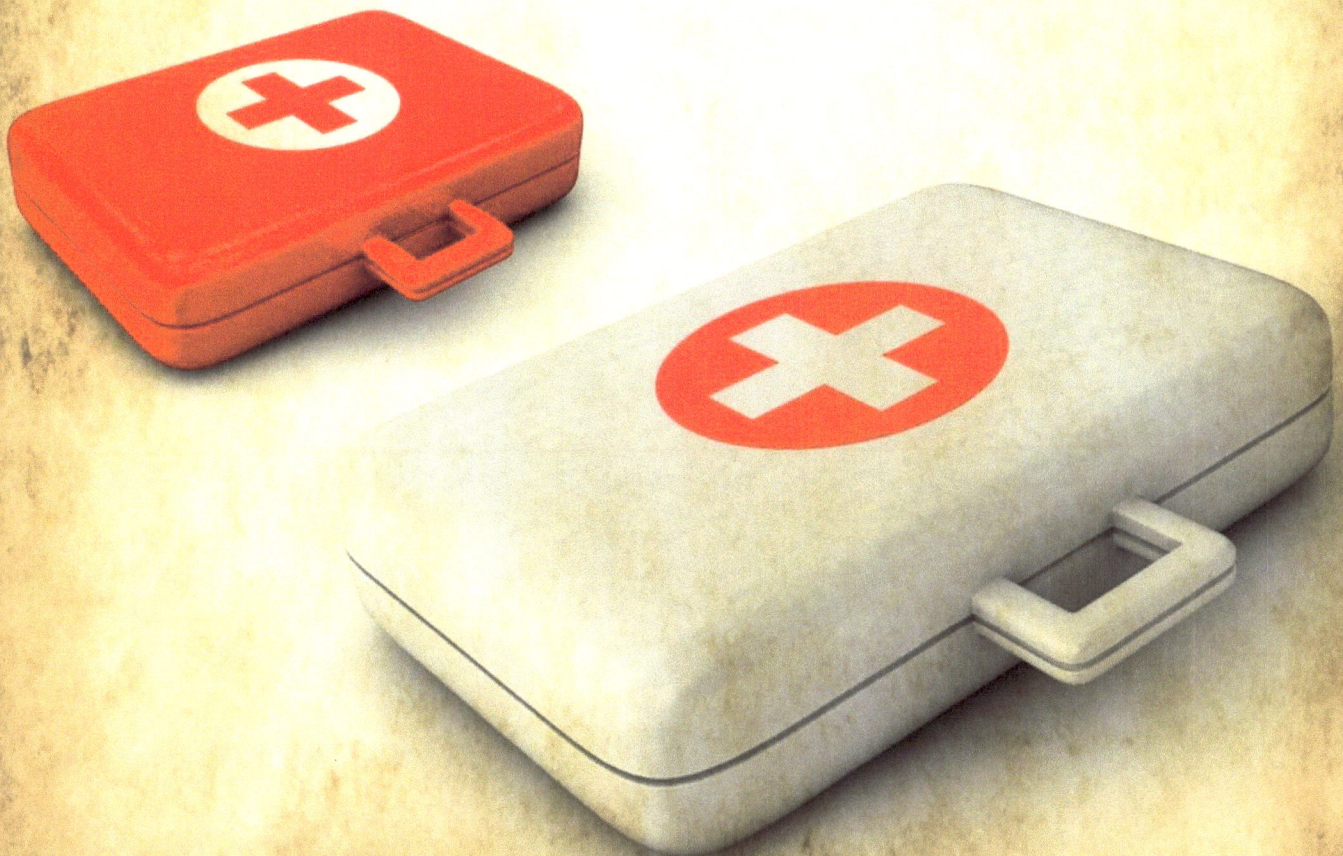

Coffee and Physical Fitness

The amounts of water, carbohydrate and salt that athletes are advised to consume during exercise are based upon their effectiveness in preventing both fatigue as well as illness due to hyperthermia, dehydration or hyper hydration. The old issues concerning coffee and caffeine were that it acts as a diuretic, thus causing more fluid loss during activity. Studies have caused researchers to re think this point. These studies suggest that consuming caffeine does not have this effect and can even have beneficial effects on keeping the body fit. Caffeine does not improve maximal oxygen capacity directly, but could permit the athlete to train at a greater power output and/or to train longer. It has also been shown to increase speed and/or power output in simulated race conditions. These effects have been found in activities that last as little as 60 seconds or as long as 2 hours. There is less information about the effects of caffeine on strength; however, recent work suggests no effect on maximal ability, but enhanced endurance or resistance to fatigue. There is no evidence that caffeine ingestion before exercise leads to dehydration, ion imbalance, or any other adverse effects.

Any Negative Effects of Coffee?

Coffee is enjoyed as a drink by millions of people worldwide. It contains caffeine, which is a mild stimulant, and in many people coffee enhances alertness, concentration and performance. Although it contains a wide variety of substances, it is generally accepted that caffeine is responsible for many of coffee's physiological effects. Because caffeine influences the central nervous system in a number of ways and because a small number of people may be particularly sensitive to these effects, some people have attributed coffee to all sorts of health problems. Caffeine is not recognized as a drug of abuse and there is no evidence for caffeine dependence. Some particularly sensitive people may suffer mild symptoms of withdrawal after sudden abstention from coffee drinking. A 150ml cup of instant coffee contains about 60mg caffeine, filtered coffee slightly more; for those who like coffee but are sensitive to caffeine, the decaffeinated beverage contains only 3mg per cup. Coffee drinking can help asthma sufferers by improving ventilator function. There is no evidence that coffee drinking is a risk for the development of cancer. For several types of cancer there is disagreement between studies but again, other aspects of lifestyle may be implicated. There is even a strong suggestion that coffee may have a protective effect against colon cancer. A possible explanation may lie in the many antioxidant substances present in coffee and which are currently subjects of active research. In some sensitive individuals, ingestion of coffee after a period of abstinence may cause a temporary rise in blood pressure but there is no hypertensive effect in the long term. Coffee made by the Scandinavian method of boiling or by the cafetiere method may cause mild elevation of plasma cholesterol concentration in some people, but instant, filter coffee, and liquid coffee extract have no such effects. Overall there is no influence of coffee drinking on heart disease risk. There is no sound scientific evidence that modest consumption of coffee has any effects on outcomes of pregnancy or on the wellbeing of the child. Bone health is not affected by coffee drinking. Adverse effects in some published studies have been attributed to aspects of lifestyle that are often shared by coffee drinkers, such as smoking and inactivity. Coffee drinking can help asthma sufferers by improving ventilator function. There is no reason for people who are prone to ulcers to avoid coffee. Research continues and must be subjected to critical scrutiny and re-evaluation. At the present time, there is no reason to forego the pleasurable experience of moderate coffee drinking for health reasons. Go ahead... Have a cup of delicious coffee!

Part - III

List of Topics

Save Your Coffee

Popular Coffee Myths Exposed

Your Own Gourmet Coffee

Save Your Coffee

So you are finally fed up with that bland black liquid, you once called coffee, brewed from the finest can of generic supermarket grinds. You are financially outraged at the price of a single cup of designer coffee shop coffee. It's now time to take matters into your own hands! So you invest in the latest technologically advanced coffee maker, including your very own coffee bean grinder. Even the engineers at NASA would envy the bells and whistles on this baby. You splurge on several pounds of the finest fresh roasted Arabica bean coffee the world has to offer. You pop open the vacuum-sealed bag and release that incredible fresh roasted coffee aroma. Your eyes widen at the site of all those shiny brown beans as you begin to grind your first pound of gourmet coffee. You feel like a mad scientist as you adjust every bell and whistle on your space age coffee maker and you revel in this accomplishment as you finish your first cup of home brewed gourmet coffee. No more long lines and outrageous prices at the neighborhood café for you! Now it's time to store all those pounds of unopened packages of fresh roasted coffee beans and the unused portion of the black gold you have just ground. Then you remember what your mother told you; "Freeze the unopened beans & Refrigerate the freshly ground coffee". At this point, it would be best if you just returned to the supermarket and purchase a stock of those generic grinds you had grown to loathe. Having the best coffee beans available and using the most advanced coffee brewing equipment will do little to provide you with the best cup of coffee you desire if the beans are not treated correctly. Looking at the facts, we learn that the natural enemies of fresh roasted coffee are light, heat and moisture. Storing your coffee away from them will keep it fresher longer. Therefore, an airtight container stored in a cool, dry, dark place is the best environment for your coffee. But why not the freezer, It's cool & dark? This does make sense, but if it be the case, then why do we not find our supermarket coffee in the frozen food section?

Here's why! ...... *Coffee is Porous !*

It is exactly this feature that allows us to use oils and syrups to flavor coffee beans for those who enjoy gourmet flavored coffees. For this same reason, coffee can also absorb flavors and moisture from your freezer. The absorbed moisture will deteriorate the natural goodness of your coffee and your expensive gourmet coffee beans will taste like your freezer. The coffee roasting process causes the beans to release their oils and essences that serve to give the coffee its distinct flavor. This is the reason why your beans are shiny. These oils are most prominent on dark-roasted coffee and espresso beans and the reason why these coffees are so distinctly flavored. The process of freezing will break down these oils and destroy the natural coffee flavor. So unless you enjoy frozen fish flavored coffee, you should avoid using the freezer to store your gourmet coffee beans at all times.

Keep moisture out! Remember, even though coffee is a natural enemy. If you have a five-pound bag of coffee to store, divide it up into smaller portions, wrap those portions up using sealable freezer bags and plastic wrap. If possible, take out the excess air from the freezer bag using a straw or a vacuum sealer. Remove the amount of coffee as you need it, and store it in an air-tight container in a cool place like your pantry.

And remember, Do not put it back into the freezer! So when is it best Refrigerate Coffee? Simply

put, Never ever, unless you are conducting a science experiment on how long it takes to ruin perfectly good coffee. The fridge is one of the absolute worst places to put coffee. The reasons why not to freeze fresh roasted coffee also apply here.

Popular Coffee Myths Exposed

Grind all beans before storing...

Absolutely wrong! Grinding the coffee breaks up the beans and their oils, exposes the beans to air, and makes the coffee go stale a lot faster, no matter how you store it. This especially holds true for flavored coffees! For the best tasting coffee, you should buy your beans whole and store them in a sealed container in a dark place. Grind right before serving!

Vacuum-sealed packaging equals fresh coffee...

Again, absolutely wrong. The coffee roasting process causes the coffee beans to release a gas by-product, specifically carbon dioxide. This gas release process continues for several days after roasting. In order to be vacuum sealed, the coffee has to first release all its CO2 or it will burst the bag, which means that it must sit around for several days before it can be packaged and shipped. This sitting around begins to rob the coffee of its freshness. Vacuum sealing is best for pre-ground coffee, which we already know is not going to taste as good as fresh-ground coffee. The best method for packaging and shipping is in valve-sealed bags. The valve allows the carbon dioxide gasses and moisture to escape but doesn't allow oxygen or moisture in. Therefore, the fresh roasted coffee beans can be packaged and shipped immediately after roasting, ensuring the coffee's freshness and taste.

Your Own Gourmet Coffee

Buy fresh roasted, whole bean coffee directly from a coffee roaster if possible

Look for valve-sealed bags, not vacuum-sealed

Store your coffee beans in a sealed container in a dark place

Grind your beans just before brewing

Part - IV

List of Topics

Brew It Better

For most of us, brewing up our morning cup of coffee is more than just a necessity, it is a matter of convenience. Each night, millions of us coffee lovers pile heaping tablespoons of our favorite gourmet coffees into those paper filters, fill the tank of our coffee makers with water and set the timer so that our coffee is ready and waiting first thing in the morning. But why would anyone spend good money on the finest gourmet coffee beans or fresh ground gourmet coffees and use just any home coffee maker. So if you are like me and you enjoy the finest gourmet and specialty coffees available, then you must also believe that they deserve the best and most reliable coffee brewing equipment available. Here is a quick list of the most popular coffee brewing methods & equipment starting from the best

French Press

The French press coffee maker (or press pot) is universally recognized as the best brewing method, allowing for the truest coffee taste and aroma. This method actually brews the coffee in the hot water (as opposed to drip machines which only pass the water through the coffee and a filter). After a few minutes of brewing, a metal filter is pressed through the brew catching the coffee grinds and then trapping them at the bottom of the carafe. What is left over is full-bodied coffee with all its aroma and essences. One of the main advantages to using a French press, other than great coffee taste, is the amount of control you have. You can control the water temperature (which incidentally should be around 190 to 200 degrees Fahrenheit, a temperature that drip makers do not achieve), you can control the amount of coffee you want to add, and you can control the brew time. Four minutes of brew time and 30 seconds of "plunging" time is considered best. Another great feature about the French press is that it is extremely portable and only requires hot water. You can take it camping or use it in places with limited kitchen space, like a boat or an RV. Some press pots can also be used to brew loose leaf teas in the same manner. As an aside, you shouldn't leave your brewed coffee in the press-pot with the grounds after you brew it! Either consume it or transfer it to a carafe, preferably a thermal carafe.

Vacuum Brewer

Vacuum brewers aren't very common, but they make coffee just about as well as a French press since the coffee and water are brewing together. A vacuum brewer has an upper and a lower chamber connected by a tube with a small filter inside. Coffee grounds are placed in the upper chamber, and water is placed in the lower chamber. As the lower chamber is heated, the water rises up to meet the coffee in the upper chamber where the brewing begins. After brewing, the water (now coffee) cools and seeps back down into the lower chamber leaving the used coffee grinds behind in the upper chamber. Ideally, the upper chamber is removed and the lower chamber is used as a decanter for the finished coffee. Vacuum brewers can be electric, stovetop, or even used over a sterno can for dramatic tabletop brewing!

The Toddy Maker

The toddy maker or Cold-Brew Coffee Maker uses an unusual cold-brewing method that creates a coffee concentrate. This concentrate is then mixed with hot water to make coffee. The concentrate can be stored in a refrigerator and used to make one cup at a time if you so desire. This method produces a low-acid coffee, which is doctor recommended for coffee drinkers with stomach conditions. Although this method of coffee brewing is sounds a bit odd, the result in taste is pleasantly surprising. One drawback is the amount of time it takes to brew. A good idea is to brew the coffee overnight. Once brewed, the concentrate can produce more than just one pot of coffee, so it's not a nightly event for a great cup of morning coffee!

Coffee **Panda**

Drip Grind Coffee Makers

Drip Grind coffee makers are the most common and usual coffee brewing method that we are familiar with. In this method, water is dripped over and passes through the coffee grinds and a filter and is caught by the coffee pot below. Despite being the most common brew method it also happens to be the one which produces a coffee brew with the least amount of flavor and aroma. There are generally 2 filter options for the drip grind coffee makers. Permanent filters: are just what they say, permanent. They are usually gold-plated so they don't add any unwanted metallic taste to your coffee, resistant to corrosion so they are dishwasher safe and economical because they don't need replacing. Permanent filters are preferred because they allow for better coffee taste as opposed to the second filter option, paper filters. Paper filters are the most common filter choice for the drip grind coffee makers. Unfortunately, paper filters can filter out more than just coffee grinds. Flavorful oils can be left behind in the filter and not make it to the finished coffee brew resulting in less coffee flavor and aroma. Since permanent filters allow for more liquid to pass through, the end result is a more flavorful cup. As you can see, the most common brew method happens to be the one which produces the least amount of coffee flavor and aroma. Since, mornings usually need to be made quick and simple, most people have never had their coffee brewed any other way. If you are one of these people, don't just splurge on gourmet coffee's, get a small French press maker, start experimenting and experience the truest coffee flavor & aroma in each cup.

Part - V

List of Topics

Secret Behind Coffee Beans

The seeds produced by the coffee plant are the coffee beans. Though these are referred to as beans they are not really beans in the true botanical sense of the word. The coffee plant bears red or purple fruits which are also called cherries or berries of coffee and the stone that lies inside is the bean which is the source of coffee. Two stones lying with their flat sides together usually constitute the coffee bean. It is from this bean that coffee is produced that can be used to produce a variety of coffee beverages like espresso, latte and cappuccino using the right coffee makers- espresso machines etc. It may be mentioned that a small percentage of any crop of coffee cherries contain a single bean in the cherries instead of the usual two. Such berries are called pea berries.

Coffee Beans Facts

Some 0.8% to 2.5% caffeine is contained in the endosperm of the coffee seed or bean. This caffeine content gives them the characteristic flavor for which the plant is cultivated. Several species of the coffee plant are there and the seeds of each species produce coffees having slightly different tastes. Variation can be observed in the flavors of different genetic subspecies also and the coffee varietals- where the coffee plants are being cultivated. Coffee beans are a major item of export of many countries. Coffee Arabica is the species that makes up the major portion (70-75%) of the world trade. The other important coffee species of coffee cultivated is the Coffee canephora. This is grown where the Coffee Arabica does not thrive.

The coffee beans are processed before they are readied for use in preparing espresso, latte, cappuccino and other special coffee drinks using coffee makers- espresso machines and the like. The processing begins with the beans being removed from the coffee cherries. The fruit is then discarded or made use of as a fertilizer. The bean or seed of coffee is then ground and used in the preparation of beverages of various kinds using a coffee maker or espresso machine.

Coffee Beans and Espresso Beans

A difference between ordinary coffee beans and the espresso beans is there. The espresso beans tend to be a concoction of beans. These are almost always a relatively dark roast like a Vienna or light French roast. This is seemingly a trade secret. So, even though the formula of the blend can be discovered the exact amounts or proportions in which the constituents are to be blended cannot be easily found out.

Flavoring of Coffee Beans

There is also the process of flavoring the coffee beans in an attempt to work upon their natural flavor to meet some purpose. Natural oils are usually used to achieve this. Half an ounce of oil is usually to be added to a pound of beans for the flavoring to be done. The primary concern of all coffee lovers being the flavor of the drinks, special attention needs to be given to ensure that the best flavor is obtained from the coffee beans. This is of crucial importance in case of preparation of espresso, cappuccino, latte and all other special coffee beverages. The superior coffee makers and espresso machines can also deliver the best results i.e. brew the perfect drinks only if the best flavored ground coffee beans are used. Many of the world class coffee makers and espresso machines of the day has been reported to be failing to deliver desirable brews owing to the use of coffee beans that were not up to the mark. The real flavor of the coffee beans starts developing with the growth of the plant and is influenced by the climate of the place where it is grown. Of course, the particular species of the coffee plant also matters in the developing of the flavor. The processing of the bean i.e. the processes that the coffee beans are made to undergo through after they are extracted from the coffee fruits also affects their taste and flavor.

Roasting for Flavors!

Roasting of the beans is an important process that helps bring out the real vibrant flavor of the beans. The carbohydrate and fat content of the coffee beans get transformed to aromatic oils by the heat of the process. This gives rise to the great coffee flavor which is cherished by the people from all corners of the world. Different types of roasting of the coffee beans also have different effects on the coffee produced i.e. varying of the composition. So, while light roast produces light flavored coffee the medium roast leads to preparation of a sweeter and fuller-bodied coffee. Again, dark roast that requires a long roasting time produces a spicy and sweet deep tasting coffee. The characteristic flavors of coffee that are a result of particular roasting are produced in the brews prepared by the coffee makers and espresso machines of the day too.

Selecting Best Coffee Beans

It is the best coffee beans that are to be selected. This is determined from the region where they are procured from. The coffee planted in a particular region and influenced by its climate produces a distinctive flavor in its cherries and beans (seeds). The Arabica coffee is considered as the very best. Gourmet coffee drinks are made using this coffee. Other varieties like the Robusta beans have been known to have more caffeine content and lesser flavor. These are also prepared cheaper. Keeping the coffee beans fresh is also very important. These are to be kept sealed in an air tight container. To take care of freshness in the coffee beverages that you make using your coffee maker or espresso machine you need to purchase whole beans of coffee from specialty shops. These beans are to be used within a week of purchase. Only then can you get to enjoy perfectly flavored coffee drink. It is always preferable to gave a good coffee grinder at home and prepare freshly ground coffee for your brewing purpose. Pre ground coffee often lacks much of the flavor and aroma that are the hallmark of premium coffee. On the other hand freshly ground coffee provides more nutritional benefit and ensures the best flavor.

Part - VI

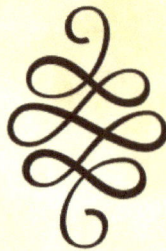

Are You a Coffee Person?

Think about a few of your personal thoughts regarding the pros and cons of drinking coffee. Have you been frightened to believe that it's horrible for you? Many people feel that coffee should be tossed in the trash like a gifted novelty condom displaying Mick Jagger's iconic tongue. There has been a coffee conundrum taking place in the past few years, with many ups and downs reported within the nutritional world. It's time to uncover and solidify the facts. Coffee has a slew of benefits. It's considered a medicinal and metabolic nutritional tool, and is a dynamic drink that you should consider incorporating into your lifestyle.

Do you remember the Folger's coffee jingle from years ago? -- "The best part of waking up, is Folgers in your cup!" -- They certainly knew how to ring the Pavlovian coffee bell of many generations due to that catchy tune and commercial. Coffee has come a long way since that brand which was first introduced in 1850. There are now tens of thousands of independent coffee houses that serve up a tasty Cup O' Joe. Coffee has received positive press about its antioxidant benefits, metabolism boosting elements, and disease protecting qualities. It has also been in the spotlight, with an unfavorable finger pointing at how it will ruin your sleep, install a new addiction to your life, and dehydrate you more than a stranded seaman. Many food items are at fault for being bad. When it comes to coffee, the individual drinking too much of it deserves to have the finger pointing at them, not the cup of coffee.

Coffee contains caffeine, which is a substance that you are probably very familiar with. Caffeine is a compound that is found in coffee plants, which acts as a stimulant to our nervous system. It's one of the more popular and legal psychoactive drugs. Our society is probably at an all time high when it comes to drinking coffee. There is no arguing that. The question lies in the quantity consumed and how this beverage is being used by the individual. Did you know that a typical cup of drip coffee has more caffeine it in than a typical double espresso drink? An 8 oz. cup of drip coffee contains between 95-200mg of caffeine, while a 1 oz. espresso typically contains 47-75mg of caffeine. According to eimportz.com, "coffee statistics show that among coffee drinkers, the average consumption in the United States is 3.1 cups of coffee per day." Yowza! That is enough caffeine to juice up a dead car battery.

When it comes to being cautious about coffee, it's simple. People who have high blood pressure, sleep issues (insomnia), and anxiety, must be mindful of coffee and what their body is displaying. Individuals who relish in coffee beer bongs every two hours just to stay motivated at work may want to consider taking it down a notch. Keep in mind that the caffeine in coffee is halved (roughly) after four to six hours. If you drink a 200mg cup of drip coffee at 3pm, this means that you can still have about 100mg of caffeine in your body at 9pm. Sleep issues beware! When coffee is enjoyed in the right way, the benefits are ten fold.

The Benefits of Coffee

It's thermogenic; produces heat, stimulates the metabolism, and helps stoke your fat burning fire. Supplies the body with Vitamin B1 and Magnesium. Both contribute to the production of energy in your body. Provides a powerful antioxidant called cholorgenic acid, which helps improve insulin sensitivity and targets free radicals. Inhibits iron (a toxic metal) absorption if sipped after a meal allows more blood to reach the brain. Say hello to creativity and work productivity! Provides the antioxidant caffeic, which has protective qualities against cancers and other diseases. Been associated with lower incidences of breast, lung, and prostate cancer. Enhances enzyme pathways in the liver, helping you detoxify estrogen. Raises nitric oxide production which improves blood vessel health (overall vascular health). Gives you a great workout boost enhancing endurance, strength, and power.

Here are some quick tips how to enjoy coffee with a healthy twist:

- Drink coffee after you have food in your stomach (coffee on an empty stomach means more adrenaline vand blood sugar imbalances)

- Enjoy coffee in the morning versus the late afternoon or evening

- Choose sipping over chugging

- Try espresso vs. drip coffee

- Test out a few organic varieties

- Become familiar with your caffeine limit (what's your jitter scale?)

- If you are a hardcore coffee lover, pick one time in the morning and another time before 2pm, if you absolutely need a second coffee boost

- Steer clear from using artificial sweeteners (Splenda, Sweet N Low, Equal)

- Use some fat (cream or coconut oil) and a sucrose based sweetener (sugar or honey). This will act as an adrenaline and blood sugar cushion

- Call a friend and schedule a social coffee shop outing once a week!

As you can see, there are a plethora of perks when it comes to the health benefits of coffee. If mainstream reporting has scared the coffee drinking bejeezus out of you, take a few steps back from the slander and hold off from kicking your cup of coffee to the curb. Recall my quick tips about how to use coffee the right way. Coffee can and should be used as a valuable beverage. Coffee provides us with pleasure and plenty of bodily protection, just like that gifted novelty condom.

Part - VII

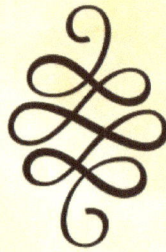

List of Topics

The Coffee Creators

The Coffee Creators

Guide Creating your own great coffee can be easy as it seems. It can be easy to not use the proper ratios, too strong or just bitter. This article will provide you some great ideas for making enjoyable coffee. You really do get what's paid for when purchasing coffee, so invest in great tools and beans and you'll always end up with the best cup of joe. Coffee has health benefits if you lay off the extras. Coffee by itself is not unhealthy, but added cream and sugar are dangerous.

- Use almond milk instead of cream and stevia for a healthy coffee.

- Don't grind whole coffee beans until just before making a fresh pot of coffee. Coffee might lose some of its flavor after being ground. Grinding it ahead of time will cause the coffee beans at once can result in weaker coffee.

Do you want to impress your guests with freshly brewed coffee? You should consider dressing up your coffee that you make by yourself. You just need a little time to start achieving floral and heart designs that will leave your friends intrigued. Try mixing up melted chocolate and milk and melt it in your coffee. Do not warm up coffee that has been previously brewed. This has been said to release harmful chemicals, as some believe. This can make coffee taste peculiar or different.

Coffee can be a great drink for anyone who works from home and need some air. Lots of coffee places offer free WiFi, which allows you to bring your work along with you as you grab a beverage and get a change of scenery. Many restaurants also now offer this service.

Test a new coffee maker before actually brewing any coffee. Run water through the machine. This will get rid of any dirt or odors that may be present in the coffee pot. Your coffee is only as great as the water you are using to make it. You might want to taste of the water before brewing with it. Put some money into a simple coffee grinder. When you grind your own beans, your coffee will maintain its aroma and flavor. Many machines give you the option to tinker with varying levels of your grind for various brewing styles. There are dozens of different ways that you can enjoy your coffee, whether you enjoy your coffee black or with all the fixings. Never keep coffee near your oven. Heat has the ability to ruin coffee's flavor very quickly.

Fair trade coffee is a great way for you the opportunity to sample something new while supporting developing nations. While it does cost a little more, the quality of coffee is worth it. You benefit children and farmers in developing countries. You can slowly cut down on how much caffeine consumption if you consume without going cold turkey. You can make your own "semi" caffeine-free brew that is ground with equal parts decaf and de-caf beans. If you use pre-ground coffee, just add however much you want of each one. Don't leave your carafe on the burner longer than 10 minutes. Use a thermos to help keep it warm. Be sure to drink coffee in moderation. Drinking too much coffee can leave you to become dehydrated. Try to drink some water as you do coffee each day. Choose a coffee machine that can do multiple things. This appliance can help you across the board when making coffee. You can set it to start at a certain time so that your coffee is brewing while you get up. This helps you get a lot of time in the morning. You will appreciate having a fresh brewed pot of worrying about making it.

Do you like having milk in coffee? There are actually a lot more choices than you have with milk when making coffee. While some people enjoy cold milk, others like to warm or froth their milk before adding it. Different kinds of milk will also offer different flavor profiles.

The ideal temperature for coffee maker is between 195 degrees to 205 degrees. Most coffee makers do not reach temperatures that hot. Try to get the water for yourself when making coffee. A simple French press also solves this problem. You can often save around a third off coffee with one. This method ensures that you avoid running out of beans on hand. Is your coffee eating into your funds? You should buy all the necessary components so you can start making your coffee at home. Brewing coffee at home also will save you easy access to a caffeine fix. Make sure you allow your coffee to completely finish its brewing cycle prior to pouring a cup. Brewing coffee is not hit its maximum flavor until the drip cycle nears its end. It isn't always easy to get the best coffee every time. By using the tips and advice you've learned here, you'll be able to enjoy the perfect cup every time.

Part - VIII

List of Topics

Misleading Myths

Multi Face Myths

Misleading Myths

Misleading Myth #1: Use Boiling Water to Make Coffee No, don't! The correct temperature for the perfect cup of coffee is 90-95 degrees C. You want hot water for optimal flavor extraction from the coffee grounds, but boiling water is too hot. Using boiling water can "over-extract" the coffee grinds, resulting in a coffee that tastes bitter. On the other hand, water that is too cold won't extract enough flavour, resulting in a flat, bland tasting cup of coffee.

Misleading Myth #2: Store your Coffee in the Fridge to Keep it Fresh No, again! Keep coffee in a cool, dry, air tight container. Coffee beans absorb moisture and moisture on the surface of the bean will leach out much of the aroma and flavour. Never store coffee in the fridge or freezer as these are moist environments. Also, coffee acts like a sponge for flavours and odours around it so storing in the fridge can cause the beans to absorb other smelly foodstuff also affecting flavour.

Misleading Myth #3: Pre-Ground Coffee Tastes Just as Good as Grinding Your Own Beans Grinding coffee beans speeds up flavour loss as the increased surface area greatly speeds up oxidization. Coffee starts losing quality almost immediately upon grinding so ground coffee should be used without delay. This is a benefit of the "bean to cup" automatic coffee machines as beans are ground immediately before brewing.

Misleading Myth #4: There is a Single Grind Level which Suits most Brewing Methods. Despite supermarket packaging of ground coffee showing it to be suitable for all sorts of brewing methods, different brewing methods actually require different grind levels. The optimal grind level is dependent on the amount of time the coffee spends in contact with water at the correct temperature. The less time in contact with water, the finer the grind needed. For example, espresso machines usually require a finer grind while a plunger requires a coarser grind. Getting the grind setting correct on your automatic espresso machine is central to a great tasting coffee.

Misleading Myth #5: You Can use Less Coffee if You Grind the Coffee Beans Finer. As mentioned above, the grind level to be used is determined by the amount of time in contact with water. Using a fine grind when a coarse grind is required, and using less of it!, will only result in a weaker taste.

Multi Face Myths

Happy-Its-Not True Myth #1: Coffee Stunts Your Growth No, coffee won't stunt your growth. This myth seems to have sprung from an early study which suggested that caffeine reduced bone mass and contributed to osteoporosis. Trouble is the subjects of the research were elderly people (and therefore not still growing!) who had calcium deficit diets. Subsequent studies have shown that there is no impact to bone density on people whose dietary intake of calcium is at recommended levels.

Happy-It's-Not True Myth #2: Coffee Causes Stomach Ulcers Stomach Ulcers are mostly caused by a bacteria called Helicobacter Pylori, with other causes being certain medications and cancer. Coffee is not linked to stomach ulcers. Recent studies have even found that stress, smoking and diet are also not causes of ulcers.

Double-Edged Myth: Coffee is Bad For You, or Coffee is Good For You There has been much published about the health pros and cons of coffee and is really the subject of another blog. However, the overriding conclusion is that normal levels of coffee drinking are not harmful to your health and may actually have some health benefits due mainly to the antioxidants found in coffee beans. And finally...

Wish-it-was-True Myth: Coffee Will Sober You Up Unfortunately, coffee does not change the alcohol content in your body and therefore cannot sober you up quicker. Coffee may make you more alert while drunk, making you think you are sober, but don't be fooled.

Part - IX

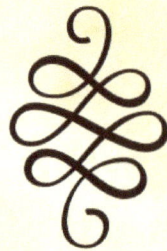

Coffee Cuisine

Intrigued by coffee cuisine? You can indulge your own culinary interests and try at home what food enthusiasts and well-seasoned cooks know already. Put on your chef hat and apron. Read about the creative recipes of famous chefs of the world. Watch videos about their cooking and, above all, go ahead and experiment. There are so many well known chefs, cooking teachers, and cookbook authors to recommend that the list is almost endless.

Emeril Lagasse

Expert in Louisiana cuisine with an extra kick. Celebrity chef Emeril Lagasse makes coffee a part of his regular repertoire. This chef shows how to discover the many ways coffee enhances the flavor of drinks, appetizers, main entrees, desserts and after-dinner beverages. Emeril's coffee recipes include: Emeril's Kicked Up Coffee Drink; Baby Back Ribs with Coffee Bourbon Barbecue Sauce; Coffee Nocello Glazed Ducks; Tiramisu with Chocolate Dipped Coffee Beans; Chicken Mole with Coffee Extract; Chocolate Coffee Flan; Blueberry Sour Cream Coffee Cake;Coffee Ice Cream Sandwich, and Spice-Rubbed Rack of Lamb with Coffee-Vanilla Sauce among others.

Bobby Flay

Food Network's celebrity chef with a best-selling Mesa Grill Cookbook featuring recipes that bring flavors and ingredients in amazing ways. Bobby Flay's southwestern style of cooking is intensely-seasoned and chile-laden. One of Bobby Flay's best recipes is a sweet and smoky beef and rib rub that blends coffee grounds, brown sugar, coriander, oregano and chili powder. This recipe is legendary in coffee cooking circles. Check it out sometime. The coffee in this recipe plays off the deep and earthy flavor of the beef but preserves a unique smokey, spicy, fragrant and a bit bitter taste that makes your taste buds sing! Other Bobby Flay's recipes include: Spiked Iced Chicory Coffee; Coffee Rubbed Flank Steak; Coffee Rub Filet with ancho chile powder; Keawe Grilled Baby Back Ribs with Kona Coffee Barbecue Grilling and Dipping Sauce, and Grilled Chocolate Coffee Steak, among others.

Jacques Pepin

Very well known chef with several appearances on PBS in several television cooking shows, including Jacques Pepin Celebrates and Fast Food My Way. Pepin's many cookbooks include Happy Cooking, Simple and Healthy Cooking, The Short-Cut Cook, A French Chef Cooks at Home, La Technique, La Methode, and others. Coffee recipes featured recently on his website: Coffee Balsamic Glaze and Fudge Coffee Brownies.

Other Chefs

Other chefs cooking with coffee include,

Wolfgang Puck: A famous Austrian television chef and author of cookbooks such as Wolfgang Puck Adventures in the Kitchen and The Wolfgang Puck Cookbook: Recipes from Spago. Wolfgang uses coffee in his cuisine extensively, especially in beverages and desserts.

Julia Child (1912-2004): Attended the famous Le Cordon Bleu cooking school after World War 2 and introduced French cuisine and cooking techniques to the American public in television programs, such as The French Chef which premiered in 1963. Julia's Gingersnap-Mocha Truffles are delicious!

Terry Conlan: Executive Chef at Lake Austin Spa Resort includes a terrific recipe featured by Epicurious called Coffee-Crusted Sirloin with Jalape⊠ed-Eye Gravy. Try it sometime!

Ke'O Velasquez: Born and raised on the Big Island of Hawaii, Ke'O Velasquez did not attend public school. Ke'O was home schooled. He attended Hawaii Community College and simply developed a cooking bug which eventually launched his career into the hospitality industry. His cooking has a unique island style which wins reluctant cooks and diners easily. A favorite recipe featured by the Food Network is Kona Coffee Crusted Rack of Lamb.

Guy Fiery: This chef is an American restaurateur, author, television personality, and game show host. He is widely known for his television series on the Food Network. Favorite coffee recipes: Java Crusted New York Steak with Stout Glaze; Coffee Bananas Foster Dessert, and Coffee Liqueur Ice Cream Pie.

The list goes on and includes Mario Batali, Paula Dean, Rachael Ray, Jacques Torres, Chef Jeffrey Blank and many others. In the end, the conclusion is quite simple. Coffee is for far more than drinking. Coffee lends itself to creative cooking ways that delight the palate and invite diners to go for seconds! Of course, to get the best results use freshly roasted quality specialty coffee preferably roasted to order from a gourmet coffee source. Lastly, remember that a good meal is not complete without a good beverage to accompany it. Coffee gives a meal that extra zing and finale that makes the moment special. It should not matter if it is a meal at home or at a commercial establishment. Be creative with coffee in your kitchen. Have fun with the beans and the brew!

Bibliography

Hilda Maria   Part – 1   Page 3

Hilda Maria is the mother of five great children. She understands the need for a great cup of coffee in a flash and enjoys using a coffee maker and fresh green coffee beans to get it.

Article Source: http://EzineArticles.com/expert/Hilda_Maria_Sigurdardottir/9411

Peter Giannakis   Part – 1   Page 3

To learn more about coffee and barista skills be sure to visit Barista Training Adelaide Or book your Adelaide Barista Courses at: Barista Courses Adelaide.

Article Source: http://EzineArticles.com/expert/Peter_Giannakis/1117282

Hilda Maria   Part – 2   Page 15

Hilda Maria is a stay at home mother of five, who enjoys writing about coffee and giving custom coffee mugs and coffee cups as gifts!

Article Source: http://EzineArticles.com/expert/Hilda_Maria_Sigurdardottir/9411

Dr Cynthia Ochi   Part – 3   Page 21

Dr. Cynthia Ochi is a coffee lover, who like you, continues her quest to find & prepare the ultimate cup of java. Her search for a quality coffee distributor led to the development of www.WeBeJava.com

Article Source: http://EzineArticles.com/expert/Cynthia_Ochi/12652

Dr Vince Manzello   Part – 4   Page 26

Dr. Vince Manzello is simply a coffee lover. His search for a quality coffee distributor led to the development of http://www.WeBeJava.com.

Article Source: http://EzineArticles.com/expert/Vince_Manzello/12571

Dene Lingard runs a web and content publishing company. This article was written with interest towards a coffee site published by Dene Lingard.

Article Source: http://EzineArticles.com/expert/Dene_Lingard/80239

Bored with repetitive mainstream run-of-the-mill health recommendations? Damian offers powerful pointers when it comes to health and wellness, giving you the ability to reach the results that you've been craving.

Article Source: http://EzineArticles.com/expert/Damian_Motlo/1935117

Pim Lorenz writes articles for EzineArticles.com. He is also a lover of coffee himself, so every word of his article is reflective of his deep emotional bonding with coffee.

Article Source: http://EzineArticles.com/expert/Pim_Lorenz/1029625

As a lover of real coffee, Angus's mission at PureBean Office Cafe is to ensure that his customers enjoy the experience of cafe quality coffee made in the convenience of the office or workplace. His office coffee machines are available for rent or sale and he also specializes in servicing offices, businesses and clubs in Sydney and Canberra areas.

Article Source: http://EzineArticles.com/expert/Angus_McPhee/1104568

So, ready to drink a delicious cup of your favorite specialty flavored Dessert and Spice Coffee or would you prefer a cup of Liqueur Flavored Coffee? Timothy ("Tim") S. Collins, the author, is called by those who know him "The Gourmet Coffee Guy." He is an expert in article writing who has done extensive research online and offline in his area of expertise, coffee marketing, as well as in other areas of personal and professional interest.

Article Source: http://EzineArticles.com/expert/Timothy_S._Collins/592011

"Be Strong"
I whispered...
...to my coffee

www.ingramcontent.com/pod-product-compliance
Lightning Source LLC
Chambersburg PA
CBHW060856270326
41934CB00003B/163